Die Räder Das Freundschaftsrennen
The Wheels The Friendship Race

Inna Nusinsky

Illustrationen von Michael Jay Roque

Illustrations by Michael Jay Roque

www.sachildrensbooks.com

First edition, 2017
Translated from English by Tess Parthum
Aus dem Englischen übersetzt von Tess Parthum

The Wheels: The Friendship race (German English Bilingual Edition)
ISBN: 978-1-5259-0236-9 paperback
ISBN: 978-1-5259-0237-6 hardcover
ISBN: 978-1-5259-0235-2 eBook

Although the author and the publisher have made every effort to ensure the accuracy and completeness of information contained in this book, we assume no responsibility for errors, inaccuracies, omission, inconsistency, or consequences from such information.

Please note that the German and English versions of the story have been written to be as close as possible. However, in some cases they differ in order to accommodate nuances and fluidity of each language.

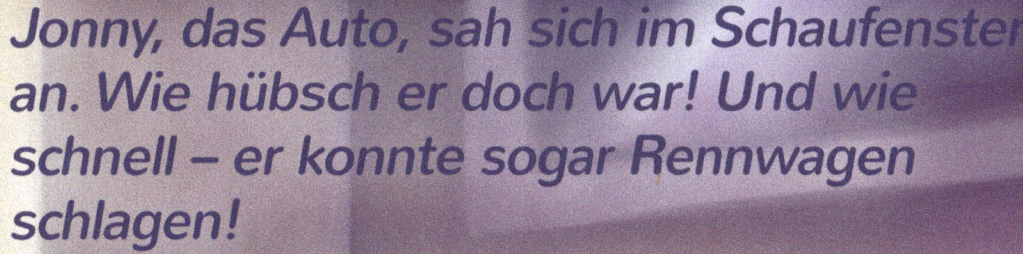

Jonny, das Auto, sah sich im Schaufenster an. Wie hübsch er doch war! Und wie schnell – er konnte sogar Rennwagen schlagen!

Jonny the car looked at himself in the shop window. How handsome he was! And what speed – he could beat even race cars!

„Ich bin der Stolz der Nachbarschaft!", rief er.

"I'm the pride of the neighborhood," he yelled.

Genau in diesem Moment unterbrachen zwei Bremsgeräusche seinen Tagtraum.

Just then, two braking sounds broke his daydream.

Plötzlich sah er ihr Spiegelbild im Glasfenster – seine Freunde Mike, das Fahrrad, und Scott, den Roller.

Suddenly, he saw them reflected in the glass window – his friends Mike the bike and Scott the scooter.

„Hey Jonny!", sagten seine Freunde. „Was gibt's?"

"Hey Jonny!" his friends said. "What's up?"

„Ich habe heute Lust auf ein kleines Rennen", sagte Jonny und plusterte seine Reifen auf. „Aber es gibt keinen, mit dem ich ein Rennen fahren könnte."

"Feeling like a little race today," said Jonny, puffing his tires. "But there's no one I can race with."

„Wir können ein Rennen mit dir fahren!", sagte Mike aufgeregt.

"We can race with you!" said Mike with excitement.

„Dafür sind Freunde da!", fügte Scott hinzu.

"That's what friends are for!" added Scott.

Jonny zeigte nicht viel Begeisterung. „Hmmm... Ein Champion braucht einen ebenbürtigen Gegner, mit dem er sich messen kann."

Jonny didn't show much enthusiasm. "Mmm... A champion needs an equal to compete with."

Mike und Scott sahen einander an. Ihre Gesichter wurden trüb.

Mike and Scott looked at each other. A cloud passed over their faces.

„Sind wir nicht gut?", fragte Mike.

"Are we not good?" asked Mike.

„Oh, ihr seid gut." Jonny schnitt eine Grimasse im Glasfenster. „Aber nicht gut genug."

"Oh, you're good," Jonny made a face in the glass window. "But not good enough."

„Ok, Jonny", sagte Scott. „Wir fordern dich jetzt sofort zu einem Rennen heraus! Lass uns die Hügelstraße hinauf fahren und schauen, wer zuerst ankommt."

"Okay, Jonny," said Scott. "We challenge you to a race right now! Let's do Hill Road and see who finishes first."

Jonny überlegte es sich grinsend.

Jonny considered it with a smirk.

Als sie die Hill Road erreichten, begann das Rennen.
As they reached Hill Road, the race began.

Es fing mit einem steilen Anstieg an. Jonny dröhnte und schaffte es in Sekunden über die Steigung.
It started with a steep climb. Jonny roared and in seconds was over the incline.

Mike, das Fahrrad, war schon auf halbem Wege... Doch der arme Roller Scott schnaufte und keuchte, während er langsam hinauffuhr.
Mike the bike was already half way... But poor Scott the scooter was huffing and puffing, slowly climbing up.

Jonny erreichte den Hügel und hielt an. Er schaute in den Rückspiegel – seine Freunde lagen weit zurück.

Jonny reached the hill and stopped. He looked at the rearview mirror – his friends were far behind.

Er war gelangweilt. Zumindest die Musik im Radio war gut! Er schloss seine Augen und fing an, sich im Takt zu bewegen.

He was bored. At least the music on the radio was good! He closed his eyes and started moving to the beat.

Plötzlich sauste etwas an ihm vorbei. Da war nur Rauch. Mike?

Suddenly, something whirred past him. There was only smoke. Mike?

Bevor er ein Wort sagen konnte, fuhr etwas anderes vorbei. Jonny schaute durch den verschwindenden Rauch—das war Scott, der voraus brauste!

Before he could say a word something else went by. Jonny looked through the disappearing smoke—that was Scott racing ahead!

Auf keinen Fall! Nun bekam er Panik. Er sollte gewinnen!

No way! Now he panicked. He should win!

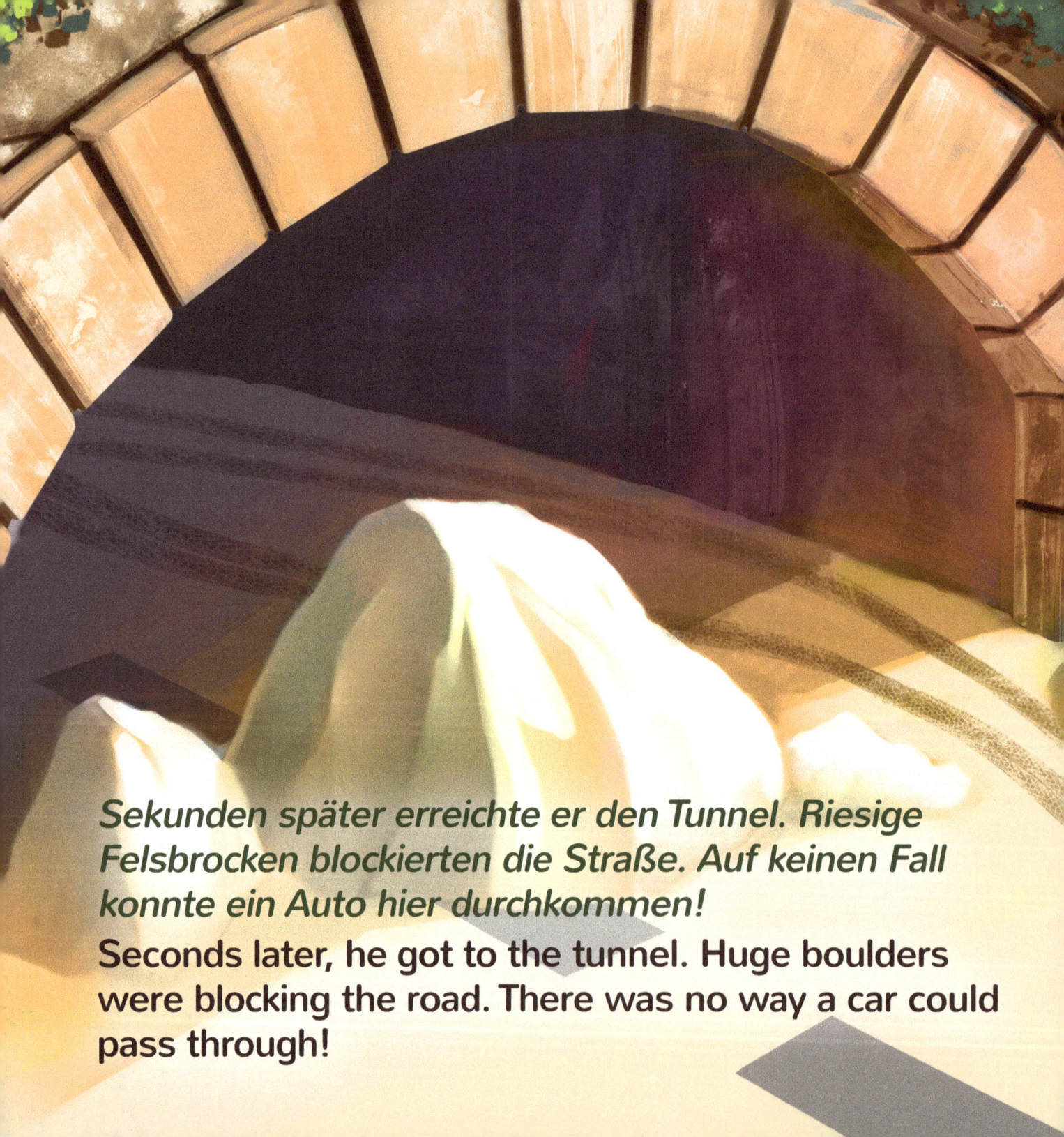

Sekunden später erreichte er den Tunnel. Riesige Felsbrocken blockierten die Straße. Auf keinen Fall konnte ein Auto hier durchkommen!

Seconds later, he got to the tunnel. Huge boulders were blocking the road. There was no way a car could pass through!

Doch dann sah er die Reifenspuren von Mike und Scott. Sie hatten sich ihren Weg um die Gesteinsbrocken herum gebahnt. Jonny seufzte.

But then, he saw the tire marks of both Mike and Scott. They had negotiated their way around the stone boulders! Jonny sighed.

In der Zwischenzeit kam Mike auf der anderen Seite des Tunnels heraus. Er lag in Führung.

Meanwhile, Mike came out on the other side of the tunnel. He was leading.

Was für ein Sieg ist das, wenn deine Freunde verlieren?, dachte er.

What kind of a win is that when your friends lose? he thought.

Innerhalb von Sekunden war Scott neben ihm.

In seconds, Scott was next to him.

„Warum hast du angehalten, Mike?", fragte er. „Du hättest das Rennen gewinnen können!"

"Why did you stop, Mike?" he asked. "You could've won the race!"

„Ja, aber... Jonny könnte dort hinten feststecken...", sagte Mike und schaute Richtung Tunnel.

"Yeah but...Jonny could be stuck back there..." said Mike, looking towards the tunnel.

Einen Moment lang schwiegen sie.
A moment of silence passed by.

*„Sollen wir zurückgehen, um nach ihm zu sehen?",
fragte Scott.*
"Shall we go to check up him?" Scott asked.

*Ein Lächeln zeigte sich auf Mikes Gesicht. „Lass uns
gehen!", rief er und drehte sich um.*
A smile formed on Mike's face. "Let's go!" he yelled
and turned back.

Am blockierten Tunnel war Jonny traurig. Nicht, weil er das Rennen verlor, sondern weil er einsam war.

At the blocked tunnel, Jonny was sad. Not because he was losing the race but because he was lonely.

Plötzlich—das Geräusche von Rädern. Das waren Scott und Mike!

Suddenly—sound of wheels. Those were Scott and Mike!

„Mike, lass uns die Felsbrocken wegschieben, damit Jonny durchfahren kann", sagte Scott.

"Mike, Let's move these boulders so Jonny can pass," said Scott.

Die Freunde fingen an, gemeinsam zu arbeiten, und schoben die Felsen aus dem Weg.

The friends started to work together, pushing the rocks out of the way.

Es war nicht einfach, doch sie schoben und schoben und bald war genug Platz, so dass Jonny sich durchzwängen konnte.

It wasn't easy, but they nudged and nudged and soon there was enough space for Jonny to squeeze through.

Kichernd erreichten sie das Ende der Hügelstraße.
Giggling, they reached the end of Hill Road.

*„Wir haben das Rennen gewonnen—wir alle!",
riefen Mike und Scott.*
"We've won the race—all of us!" exclaimed Mike
and Scott.

Nur Jonny war still. „Ich habe mich euch gegenüber schlecht benommen", gab er zu. „Ich habe es spät begriffen, Leute, dass wir gemeinsam viel mehr tun können. Danke, meine Freunde, dass ihr mir geholfen habt, das zu verstehen!"

Only Jonny was quiet. "I behaved badly with you," he admitted. "I realized it late, guys that together we can do much more. Thank you, my friends, for helping me understand that!"

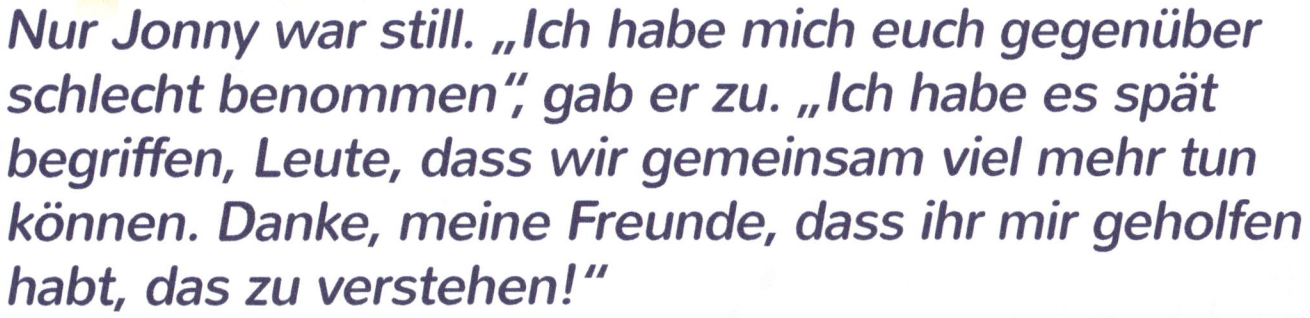

Plötzlich gab es Applaus und Jubel für diese wunderbare Gruppe von drei tollen Freunden...

Suddenly, there was applause, cheering for this wonderful bunch of three terrific friends...

Freunde, die entdeckten, dass keiner von ihnen so gut war wie sie alle.

Friends who discovered that none of them was as good as all of them.